poetry speaks
who i am

EDITOR: **ELISE PASCHEN**
SERIES EDITOR:
DOMINIQUE RACCAH

ADVISORY EDITORS:
elizabeth alexander
joy harjo
brad leithauser

sourcebooks
jabberwocky

Published by Sourcebooks Jabberwocky, an imprint of Sourcebooks, Inc.
P.O. Box 4410, Naperville, Illinois 60567-4410
(630) 961-3900
Fax: (630) 961-2168
www.jabberwockykids.com

Library of Congress Cataloging-in-Publication Data

Poetry speaks who I am / edited by Elise Paschen and Dominique Raccah.
p. cm.
Includes bibliographical references and index.
1. American poetry. 2. English poetry. I. Paschen, Elise. II. Raccah, Dominique.
PS584.P63 2010
811'.008--dc22
2010032964

Source of Production: Bang Printing, Brainerd, Minnesota, USA
Date of Production: August 2017
Run Number: 5010283

Printed and bound in the United States of America.
BG 16 15 14

CONTENTS

ON THE CD

POEM TITLES/TRACK NUMBERS

ABOUT THE AUDIO CD

This audio CD includes:

- **47** tracks

- **44** poems read by **35** poets. Most are read by the poets themselves. Use the Index at the back to find your favorite poems and poets.

- **33** poets, past and present, reading their own work.

- **39** original poem recordings—you'll only find them here in *Poetry Speaks Who I Am*

We hope you'll listen to the CD while you read the book—or enjoy it all on its own.

A NOTE FROM THE PUBLISHER

There are extraordinary poems in *Poetry Speaks Who I Am*. We asked some of the most talented poets in the country to share with us the poems that had touched them when they were your age and the poems they have written that they thought could mean something important to you. It is a highly unusual collection—coming-of-age moments caught next to classics next to grieving, kitchen tables, Cinderella, dragons, and school periods.

I started keeping a poetry notebook when I was in eighth grade. It had all of my favorite poems, and I think I kept a version of that notebook well into my twenties. I would go back to it to find the poems that moved me (some of those poems even came through our amazing Advisory Board all the way to this book).

So *Poetry Speaks Who I Am* is a highly personal book. For me, this poetry is life altering. It's gritty. It's difficult. And it hurts in all the ways that growing hurts. It's meant to be visceral and immediate. It's meant to be experienced. So we paired the book with an audio CD on which you can hear how the poets themselves interpret these poems. Like all of the Poetry Speaks books I've made, the book was many years in the making. And poets have been recording tracks for the disc for nearly a year.

One of the things I found interesting when I conceptualized the book—the feel of it and the voices that would create it—was that there wasn't a poetry book made for you. In fact, we seem to skip from great poetry books for young children directly to adult poetry. And yet, it's at your age that poetry can rock your soul because these poets are talking about all the things that you're feeling and feeling deeply. So this is our hope. Not only to bring you a book that touches and moves you, that speaks directly to you, but also to bring you a book that inspires you to try writing and expressing your own poetry.

And in the end, poetry changes the world because, as poet Jason Shinder says beautifully in *Eternity*—the poem that begins this book—it makes us feel known:

> *And every time the poem is read,*
>
> *no matter what her situation or age,*
>
> *this is more or less what happens.*

Poetry moves you when it's true. Find what's true for you. Happy hunting.

—Dominique Raccah

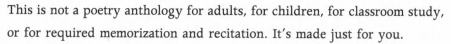

INTRODUCTION

This is not a poetry anthology for adults, for children, for classroom study, or for required memorization and recitation. It's made just for you.

When I was younger, I wish I had possessed an anthology like this one—a compilation that brings poetry to life through words and recordings. In grammar school, I memorized the poems I discovered in a favorite poetry anthology my parents had given me. In high school, after my British Literature teacher introduced me to the work of William Butler Yeats, I began to understand how to write a poem. But in middle school there were no poetry anthologies compiled just for students and poetry was not taught in class. So I gravitated toward poets of the past and read William Shakespeare's love sonnets, trying to imitate them. I had no idea that poets were alive and writing. This anthology attempts to fill that void by offering poems about subjects that might express what's on your mind.

Youth inspires poets. So when we asked poets to send poems either that were important to them at your age or that they'd written about *being* your age, we received hundreds of submissions. Many writers try to capture those moments you may be thinking about now as you step into a new world.

We strived to create an anthology where you can discover poems about the changes taking place in your life. We offer first kiss poems like "Zodiac" or "The Skokie Theatre." If you've ever stood in the outfield, waiting to catch a fly ball, check out "Baseball." There are some Bar Mitzvah poems called "33" and "49." Poems about changing bodies such as "Bra Shopping." Poems about the times you think you hate your mother as in "The Adversary" and poems about loving her such as "Dear Mama (4)." Poems about loneliness like Robert Frost's "Acquainted with the Night." We even have a "Vampire Serenade." There are poems about navigating the turbulence of friendship like "Caroline" or the riptides of your parents' marriage as in "Mediation." We have paired classic poems with contemporary poems, from John Keats to Toi Derricotte, so you can read how poets throughout the ages have mulled over the same subjects.

Some poems will help you catch your breath, others will let you slowly exhale.

Many of the poets traveled to studios to record their poems for *Poetry Speaks Who I Am*. When you listen to the CD, you will hear the immediacy of their words and the nuance of expression, and you will be able to hear and perhaps understand the poem from the poet's perspective.

In seventh grade, my friends and I would get together at each other's houses, listening for long afternoons to our favorite records. Older siblings introduced us to Carly Simon, James Taylor, Carole King, and we would sit and talk and sometimes just sit and listen to the songs, memorizing each one, playing them over and over in our minds. Let's hope that these poem recordings touch that same nerve for you and that they hold the same power that music did.

Throughout my life, whenever I read a book I often scribble down a draft of a poem in the back pages. In *Poetry Speaks Who I Am*, you will find pages at the end where you can write down your own thoughts. Maybe some of the poems in this anthology will stir you to write some poems of your own.

We hope you will find inspiring company with these poems and with these poets. As the German poet Rainer Maria Rilke writes: "Live a while in these books…" So live a while with these poems.

—Elise Paschen

ETERNITY

jason shinder

A poem written three thousand years ago

about a man who walks among horses
grazing on a hill under the small stars

comes to life on a page in a book

and the woman reading the poem
in her kitchen filled with a gold, metallic light

find the experience of living in that moment

so vividly described as to make her feel known
to another; until the woman and the poet share

not only their souls but the exact silence

between each word. And every time the poem is read,
no matter what her situation or age,

this is more or less what happens.

PERHAPS THE WORLD ENDS HERE

joy harjo » track 1 read by the poet

The world begins at a kitchen table. No matter what, we must eat to live.

The gifts of earth are brought and prepared, set on the table. So it has been since creation, and it will go on.

We chase chickens or dogs away from it. Babies teethe at the corners. They scrape their knees under it.

It is here that children are given instructions on what it means to be human. We make men at it, we make women.

At this table we gossip, recall enemies and the ghosts of lovers.

Our dreams drink coffee with us as they put their arms around our children. They laugh with us at our poor falling-down selves and as we put ourselves back together once again at the table.

This table has been a house in the rain, an umbrella in the sun.

Wars have begun and ended at this table. It is a place to hide in the shadow of terror. A place to celebrate the terrible victory.

We have given birth on this table, and have prepared our parents for burial here.

At this table we sing with joy, with sorrow. We pray of suffering and remorse. We give thanks.

Perhaps the world will end at the kitchen table, while we are laughing and crying, eating of the last sweet bite.

STILL I RISE

maya angelou

You may write me down in history
With your bitter, twisted lies,
You may trod me in the very dirt
But still, like dust, I'll rise.

Does my sassiness upset you?
Why are you beset with gloom?
'Cause I walk like I've got oil wells
Pumping in my living room.

Just like moons and like suns,
With the certainty of tides,
Just like hopes springing high,
Still I'll rise.

Did you want to see me broken?
Bowed head and lowered eyes?
Shoulders falling down like teardrops.
Weakened by my soulful cries.

Does my haughtiness offend you?
Don't you take it awful hard
'Cause I laugh like I've got gold mines
Diggin' in my own back yard.

You may shoot me with your words,
You may cut me with your eyes,
You may kill me with your hatefulness,
But still, like air, I'll rise.

Does my sexiness upset you?
Does it come as a surprise
That I dance like I've got diamonds
At the meeting of my thighs?

Out of the huts of history's shame
I rise
Up from a past that's rooted in pain
I rise
I'm a black ocean, leaping and wide,
Welling and swelling I bear in the tide.
Leaving behind nights of terror and fear
I rise
Into a daybreak that's wondrously clear
I rise
Bringing the gifts that my ancestors gave,
I am the dream and the hope of the slave.
I rise
I rise
I rise.

CINDERELLA'S DIARY

ron koertge

I miss my stepmother. What a thing to say
but it's true. The prince is so boring: four
hours to dress and then the cheering throngs.
Again. The page who holds the door is cute
enough to eat. Where is he once Mr. Charming
kisses my forehead goodnight?

Every morning I gaze out a casement window
at the hunters, dark men with blood on their
boots who joke and mount, their black trousers
straining, rough beards, callused hands, selfish,
abrupt...

Oh, dear diary—I am lost in ever after:
Those insufferable birds, someone in every
room with a lute, the queen calling me to look
at another painting of her son, this time
holding the transparent slipper I wish
I'd never seen.

VAMPIRE'S SERENADE

dana gioia » **track 2** read by the poet

(Aria from *Nosferatu*)

I am the image that darkens your glass,
The shadow that falls wherever you pass.
I am the dream you cannot forget,
The face you remember without having met.

I am the truth that must not be spoken,
The midnight vow that cannot be broken.
I am the bell that tolls out the hours.
I am the fire that warms and devours.

I am the hunger that you have denied,
The ache of desire piercing your side.
I am the sin you have never confessed,
The forbidden hand caressing your breast.

You've heard me inside you speak in your dreams,
Sigh in the ocean, whisper in streams.
I am the future you crave and you fear.
You know what I bring. Now I am here.

ALONE

edgar allan poe

From childhood's hour I have not been
As others were; I have not seen
As others saw; I could not bring
My passions from a common spring.
From the same source I have not taken
My sorrow; I could not awaken
My heart to joy at the same tone;
And all I loved, I loved alone.
Then—in my childhood, in the dawn
Of a most stormy life—was drawn
From every depth of good and ill
The mystery which binds me still:
From the torrent, or the fountain,
From the red cliff of the mountain,
From the sun that round me rolled
In its autumn tint of gold,
From the lightning in the sky
As it passed me flying by,
From the thunder and the storm,
And the cloud that took the form
(When the rest of Heaven was blue)
Of a demon in my view.

ALONE

siegfried sassoon

"When I'm alone"—the words tripped off his tongue
As though to be alone were nothing strange.
"When I was young," he said; "when I was young…"

I thought of age, and loneliness, and change.
I thought how strange we grow when we're alone,
And how unlike the selves that meet and talk,
And blow the candles out, and say good night.

Alone…The word is life endured and known.
It is the stillness where our spirits walk
And all but inmost faith is overthrown.

CAROLINE

allison joseph

In eighth grade, we teased that girl
as much as we could, mocking

her clothes, her stringy hair,
her flat, pallid face that revealed

little protest. Used to being
the one white girl in our class

of blacks, Hispanics, she endured
our taunts on her lack of rhythm,

on her stiff, flat-butted walk.
How we pitied her—brown hair

parted straight, pulled back
in a dull ponytail, her jeans

or corduroy pants in washed-out
shades of gray or blue,

her homework neatly done
in pained, legible print.

How weak it was to be white,
we thought, not able to dance

or run fast, to have skin
that peeled from too much sun.

We never let Caroline forget
that she was white and we

were black, that we could
swing our hips and snap

our fingers without trying,
privy to street-slang rhythms.

But she was our white girl,
and if anyone else dared

to touch her or call her names,
we'd be on them in a second,

calling them ugly right back,
slapping offenders if necessary.

With one of us by her side,
she could walk the school

safely, knowing she was ours
even if we didn't let her in

all the way, even if we laughed
at her white speech, thin lips.

rosellen brown

What are friends for, my mother asks.
A duty undone, visit missed,
casserole unbaked for sick Jane.
Someone has just made her bitter.

Nothing. They are for nothing, friends,
I think. All they do in the end—
they *touch* you. They fill you like music.

I LOVED MY FRIEND

langston hughes

I loved my friend.
He went away from me.
There's nothing more to say.
The poem ends,
Soft as it began—
I loved my friend.

IN THE FIFTH-GRADE LOCKER ROOM

rebecca lauren » track 3 read by the poet

We removed our sports bras through gym shirt sleeves
faced gray lockers like criminals, busied ourselves
with intricate straps and hooks, stole
glances at forbidden skin on either side.

Parts of us were rounding, sprouting
hair. We'd learned in secret to use razors,
to pack pads in our knapsacks and bleed
discreetly, posing as boys as long as we could.

Shower stalls glared at our backs with steely eyes,
dared any of us to perform a preemptive
striptease, to stand as the 3-D diagram
of how bodies should be developing now.

Even after the long, sweaty mile on the track
no one ever volunteered, except Janet. She was slow,
shut up in a dark closet for days at a time before we were born
with no way to break the locks on her mind.

I imagine she swung from plastic hangers
until they snapped, dressed herself in coats—
layered peacoat over raincoat over windbreaker
to keep out the shadows that told her not to cry.

Now barefoot, she braved the tiled shower floor alone
and when her breasts flopped freely, we aimed to look
away but the preview of what was to come
stood before us, mouth gaping to the spray.

BRA SHOPPING

parneshia jones » track 4 read by the poet

Saturday afternoon, Marshall Fields, 2nd floor, women's lingerie department

Mama and I enter into no man's, and I mean no man in sight, land
of frilly lace, night gowns, grandma panties, and support everything.

A wall covered with hundreds of white bras, some with lace, ribbons,
and frills like party favors, as if bras are cause for celebration.

Some have these dainty ditsy bows in the middle.
That's a nice accent don't you think? Mama says. *Isn't that cute?*
Like a dumb bow in the middle of the bra will take away some of the
attention from two looming, bulging issues.

Suddenly, a little woman with glasses attached to a chain around her neck,
who cares way too much about bras appears. *What size is she?* She asks.
You want something with support honey, winking at me.
My mother looks straight at my chest. *Oh she's good size. She's out of that
training bra phase. I want her to have a bra that will hold them in proper.*

Them, them she says, like they're two midgets I keep strapped to my chest.
I stand there while these two women, one my own kin, discuss the
maintenance and storage of my two dependents.

We enter the dressing room where mirrors are waiting to laugh
at me. There are women running in and out, half-naked,
with things showing that I hope never to see on my own body.

I stand there wasting away in a sea of bras, feeling like a rag doll under
interrogation with mama on one side and the bra woman on the other,
fixing straps, poking me, snapping the back, underwire begins to dig
my breasts a grave. The bra shapes my breasts into pristine bullets.
No movement, no pulse, no life, they just sit there like shelves.

After we are half-way through the bra inventory we check-out.
Oh honey, you picked some beautiful bras. The bra lady says.
Remember, hand wash. How about burned and buried, I think to myself.

The bra lady and my mother discuss how the bras fit just right
and will do the trick with no bouncing at all. Mama thanks the lady
for *torturing* me and we leave the nightmare that is the bra department.
My mother turns and looks at me. *Now really, was that so bad?*

BLOOD CHARM

annie finch » track 5 read by the poet

How can I listen to the moon?
Your blood will listen, like a charm.

I knew a way to feel the sun
as if a statue felt warm eyes.
Even with ruins on the moon,
your blood will listen, every time.

Now I am the one with eyes.
Your blood can listen, every time.

PAUSE

nikki grimes

The sky is slate
and the world is a cold
and slushy place till
Kiara stops by Video Haven,
sunshine in jeans
and knee-high boots.
"Hey, Keys.
I see you're working hard.
Make sure you stack those videos
in alphabetical order."
I smile as if
it's my invention.
The manager cuts his eyes at me,
so I keep moving.
My part-time shift
runs another hour.
"Catch you later,"
I tell her,
and she blows me a kiss
warm enough to melt
every patch of ice
on the planet.
Gotta watch out
for the sun.

THE DELIGHT SONG OF TSOAI-TALEE

n. scott momaday

I am a feather on the bright sky
I am the blue horse that runs in the plain
I am the fish that rolls, shining, in the water
I am the shadow that follows a child
I am the evening light, the lustre of meadows
I am an eagle playing with the wind
I am a cluster of bright beads
I am the farthest star
I am the cold of dawn
I am the roaring of the rain
I am the glitter on the crust of the snow
I am the long track of the moon in a lake
I am a flame of four colors
I am a deer standing away in the dusk
I am a field of sumac and the pomme blanche
I am an angle of geese in the winter sky
I am the hunger of a young wolf
I am the whole dream of these things
You see, I am alive, I am alive
I stand in good relation to the earth
I stand in good relation to the gods
I stand in good relation to all that is beautiful
I stand in good relation to the daughter of Tsen-tainte
You see, I am alive, I am alive.

INDIAN EDUCATION

sherman alexie

Crazy Horse came back to life
in a storage room in the Smithsonian,
his body rising from a wooden crate
mistakenly marked ANONYMOUS HOPI MALE.

Crazy Horse wandered the halls, found
the surface of the moon, Judy Garland
and her red shoes, a stuffed horse named
Comanche, the only surviving

member of the Seventh Cavalry
at Little Big Horn. Crazy Horse was found
in the morning by a security guard
who took him home and left him alone

in a room with cable television. Crazy Horse
watched a basketball game, every black and white
western, a documentary about a scientist
who travelled the Great Plains in the 1800s

measuring Indians and settlers, discovering
that the Indians were two inches taller
on average, and in some areas, the difference
in height exceeded a foot, which proved nothing

although Crazy Horse measured himself
against the fact of a mirror, traded faces
with a taxi driver and memorized the city,
folding, unfolding, his mapped heart.

ONE ART

elizabeth bishop

The art of losing isn't hard to master;
so many things seem filled with the intent
to be lost that their loss is no disaster.

Lose something every day. Accept the fluster
of lost door keys, the hour badly spent.
The art of losing isn't hard to master.

Then practice losing farther, losing faster:
places, and names, and where it was you meant
to travel. None of these will bring disaster.

I lost my mother's watch. And look! my last, or
next-to-last, of three loved houses went.
The art of losing isn't hard to master.

I lost two cities, lovely ones. And, vaster,
some realms I owned, two rivers, a continent.
I miss them, but it wasn't a disaster.

—Even losing you (the joking voice, a gesture
I love) I shan't have lied. It's evident
the art of losing's not too hard to master
though it may look like (*Write* it!) like disaster.

HERE

arthur sze » **track 6** read by the poet

Here a snail on a wet leaf shivers and dreams of spring.

Here a green iris in December.

Here the topaz light of the sky.

Here one stops hearing a twig break and listens for deer.

Here the art of the ventriloquist.

Here the obsession of a kleptomaniac to steal red pushpins.

Here the art of the alibi.

Here one walks into an abandoned farmhouse and hears a tarantella.

Here one dreamed a bear claw and died.

Here a humpback whale leaped out of the ocean.

Here the outboard motor stopped but a man made it to this island with one oar.

Here the actor forgot his lines and wept.

Here the art of prayer.

Here marbles, buttons, thimbles, dice, pins, stamps, beads.

Here one becomes terrified.

Here one wants to see as a god sees and becomes clear amber.

Here one is clear pine.

HAIKU

sonia sanchez » track 7 read by the poet

(written from Peking)

let me wear the day
well so when it reaches you
you will enjoy it

GOOD GIRL

molly peacock » tracks 8 & 9 read by the poet

Hold up the universe, good girl. Hold up
the tent that is the sky of your world at which
you are the narrow center pole, good girl. Rup-
ture is the enemy. Keep all whole. The itch
to be yourself, plump and bending, below a sky
unending, held up by God forever
is denied by you as Central Control. Sever
yourself, poor false Atlas, poor "Atlesse," lie
recumbent below the sky. Nothing falls down,
except you, luscious and limited on the ground.
Holding everything up, always on your own,
creates a loneliness so profound
you are nothing but a column, good girl,
a temple ruin against a sky held up
by forces beyond you. Let yourself curl
up: a fleshy foetal figure cupped
about its own vibrant soul. You are
the universe about its pole. God's not far.

BAD BOATS

laura jensen

They are like women because they sway.
They are like men because they swagger.
They are like lions because they are king here.
They walk on the sea. The drifting
logs are good: they are taking their punishment.
But the bad boats are ready to be bad,
to overturn in water, to demolish the swagger
and the sway. They are bad boats
because they cannot wind their own rope
or guide themselves neatly close to the wharf.
In their egomania they are glad
for the burden of the storm the men are shirking
when they go for their coffee and yawn.
They are bad boats and they hate their anchors.

NO IMAGES

waring cuney

She does not know
her beauty,
she thinks her brown body
has no glory.

If she could dance
naked
under palm trees
and see her image in the river,
she would know.

But there are no palm trees
on the street,
and dish water gives back
no images.

WON'T YOU CELEBRATE WITH ME

lucille clifton

won't you celebrate with me
what i have shaped into
a kind of life? i had no model.
born in babylon
both nonwhite and woman
what did i see to be except myself?
i made it up
here on this bridge between
starshine and clay,
my one hand holding tight
my other hand; come celebrate
with me that everyday
something has tried to kill me
and has failed.

WHAT I'M TELLING YOU

elizabeth alexander » track 10 read by the poet

If I say, my father was Betty Shabazz's lawyer, the poem can
go no further. I've given you the punchline. If you know
who she is, all you can think about is how and what you
want to know about me, about my father, about Malcolm,
especially in 1990 when he's all over t-shirts and medallions,
but what I'm telling you is that Mrs. Shabazz was a nice
lady to me, I loved her name for the wrong reasons,
SHABAZZ! and what I remember is going to visit her
daughters in 1970 in a dark house with little furniture and
leaving with a candy necklace the daughters gave me, to
keep. Now that children see his name and call him Malcolm
Ten, and someone called her Mrs. Ex-es, and they don't
really remember who he was or what he said or how he
smiled the way it happened when it did, and neither do I,
I think about how history is made more than what happened
and about a nice woman in a dark house filled with
daughters and candy, something dim and unspoken,
expectation.

HOW I LEARNED TO SWEEP

julia alvarez

My mother never taught me sweeping...
One afternoon she found me watching
t.v. She eyed the dusty floor
boldly, and put a broom before me, and said she'd like to be able
to eat her dinner off that table,
and nodded at my feet, then left.
I knew right off what she expected
and went at it. I stepped and swept:
The t.v. blared the news; I kept
my mind on what I had to do,
until in minutes, I was through.
Her floor was as immaculate
as a just-washed dinner plate.
I waited for her to return
and turned to watch the President,
live from the White House, talk of war:
in the Far East our soldiers were
landing in their helicopters

into jungles their propellers
swept like weeds seen underwater
while perplexing shots were fired
from those beautiful green gardens
into which these dragonflies
filled with little men descended.
I got up and swept again
as they fell out of the sky
I swept all the harder when
I watched a dozen of them die...
as if their dust fell through the screen
upon the floor I had just cleaned.
She came back and turned the dial;
the screen went dark. *That's beautiful,*
she said, and ran her clean hand through
my hair, and on, over the windowsill, coffee table, rocker, desk,
and held it up—I held my breath—
That's beautiful, she said, impressed,
she hadn't found a speck of death.

SONNET 130

william shakespeare

My mistress' eyes are nothing like the sun;
Coral is far more red than her lips' red;
If snow be white, why then her breasts are dun;
If hairs be wires, black wires grow on her head.
I have seen roses damasked, red and white,
But no such roses see I in her cheeks;
And in some perfumes is there more delight
Than in the breath that from my mistress reeks.
I love to hear her speak, yet well I know
That music hath a far more pleasing sound;
I grant I never saw a goddess go;
My mistress, when she walks, treads on the ground.
   And yet, by heaven, I think my love as rare
   As any she belied with false compare.

LITANY

billy collins » track 11 read by the poet

You are the bread and the knife,
The crystal goblet and the wine...
—Jacques Crickillon

You are the bread and the knife,
the crystal goblet and the wine.
You are the dew on the morning grass
and the burning wheel of the sun.
You are the white apron of the baker,
and the marsh birds suddenly in flight.

However, you are not the wind in the orchard,
the plums on the counter,
or the house of cards.
And you are certainly not the pine-scented air.
There is just no way that you are the pine-scented air.

It is possible that you are the fish under the bridge,
maybe even the pigeon on the general's head,
but you are not even close
to being the field of cornflowers at dusk.

And a quick look in the mirror will show
that you are neither the boots in the corner
nor the boat asleep in its boathouse.

It might interest you to know,
speaking of the plentiful imagery of the world,
that I am the sound of rain on the roof.

I also happen to be the shooting star,
the evening paper blowing down an alley
and the basket of chestnuts on the kitchen table.

I am also the moon in the trees
and the blind woman's tea cup.
But don't worry, I'm not the bread and the knife.
You are still the bread and the knife.
You will always be the bread and the knife,
not to mention the crystal goblet and—somehow—the wine.

A TEENAGE COUPLE

brad leithauser

He said, or she said
(Desperate to have their say),
You know, we may not last forever....
And on that unthinkable day

(She said, or he said—
Somebody *needed* to know),
Who will be the last to turn and look
After we've agreed to go

Our separate ways?
(Which one, that is, will be the one
To watch the other hobbling off,
Black against the sun?)

FREE PERIOD

david yezzi » track 12 read by the poet

Outside study hall,
it's me, my girlfriend, and a guy
named Rob—bony kid, klutzy
at games, fluent in French.
He's behind her;

I'm asleep or half
asleep (it's morning), and, as I
squint into the trapezoid of light
breaking on the bench and me,
I see him raise

his hand to her head
from the back, so gently
she doesn't notice
him at first, but stands there,
carved in ebony

and beaten gold:
Stacey's straight black hair
falling in shafts of sun.
He smoothes it down,
firmly now,

so that she turns,
kind of freaked, as if to say,
"Can you believe it?"
to me still coming to.
Yes, I guess I can,

I think to myself,
with only a twinge
of jealousy, with admiration,
actually. And pity—since he'd seen
beauty raw,

for which humiliation
was the smallest price,
and, dazzled, grasped at it,
not getting hold.
It wasn't his, god knows,

or mine, as I,
months later, learned
hopelessly—almost fatally,
it felt—or even hers, though it was
of her and around her,

in that freeze-frame
of low sunshine,
with us irremediably young
and strung-out from love
and lack of love.

ZODIAC

elizabeth alexander » **track 13** read by the poet

You kissed me once and now I wait for more.
We're standing underneath a swollen tree.
A bridge troll waits to snatch me if I cross.
Your bicycle handles are rusted blue.

My mouth has lost its flavor from this kiss.
I taste of warm apple. My lips are fat.
If these blossoms fall they'll mark our faces:
Gold shards of pollen or flower-shaped dents.

Is it bird wings that bat between my legs?
Is there a myth for trolls? Bulfinch says no.
My mother has a friend who reads the stars.
I am fourteen. "My dear, you look in love."

Your fingers stained dull orange from the bike.
Svetlana eyes and hands, no crystal ball.
White ripe blossoms on a trembling tree.
Again, I think. *I want you to kiss me.*

THE SKOKIE THEATRE

edward hirsch » track 14 read by the poet

Twelve years old and lovesick, bumbling
and terrified for the first time in my life,
but strangely hopeful, too, and stunned,
definitely stunned—I wanted to cry,
I almost started to sob when Chris Klein
actually touched me—oh God—below the belt
in the back row of the Skokie Theatre.
Our knees bumped helplessly, our mouths
were glued together like flypaper, our lips
were grinding in a hysterical grimace
while the most handsome man in the world
twitched his hips on the flickering screen
and the girls began to scream in the dark.

I didn't know one thing about the body yet,
about the deep foam filling my bones,
but I wanted to cry out in desolation
when she touched me again, when the lights
flooded on in the crowded theatre
and the other kids started to file
into the narrow aisles, into a lobby
of faded purple splendor, into the last
Saturday in August before she moved away.
I never wanted to move again, but suddenly
we were being lifted toward the sidewalk
in a crush of bodies, blinking, shy,
unprepared for the ringing familiar voices
and the harsh glare of sunlight, the brightness
of an afternoon that left us gripping
each other's hands, trembling and changed.

VALENTINE

wendy cope

My heart had made its mind up
And I'm afraid it's you.
Whatever you've got lined up,
my heart has made its mind up
And if you can't be signed up
This year, next year will do.
My heart has made its mind up
And I'm afraid it's you.

AN ANGRY VALENTINE

myra cohn livingston

If you won't be my Valentine
I'll *scream*, I'll *yell*, I'll *bite*!
I'll cry aloud, I'll start to pine
If you won't be my Valentine.
I'll frown and fret, I'll mope and whine,
And it will serve you right—
If you won't be my Valentine
I'll *scream*, I'll *yell*, I'll *bite*!

WHAT GREAT GRIEF HAS MADE THE EMPRESS MUTE

NY TIMES HEADLINE

june jordan

Because it was raining outside the palace
Because there was no rain in her vicinity

Because people kept asking her questions
Because nobody ever asked her anything

Because marriage robbed her of her mother
Because she lost her daughters to the same tradition

Because her son laughed when she opened her mouth
Because he never delighted in anything she said

Because romance carried the rose inside a fist
Because she hungered for the fragrance of the rose

Because the jewels of her life did not belong to her
Because the glow of gold and silk disguised her soul

Because nothing she could say could change the melted
  music of her space
Because the privilege of her misery was something she could
  not disgrace

Because no one could imagine reasons for her grief
Because her grief required no imagination

Because it was raining outside the palace
Because there was no rain in her vicinity

Dedicated to The Empress Michiko
and to Janice Mirikitani

MAD GIRL'S LOVE SONG

sylvia plath

I shut my eyes and all the world drops dead;
I lift my lids and all is born again.
(I think I made you up inside my head.)

The stars go waltzing out in blue and red,
And arbitrary blackness gallops in:
I shut my eyes and all the world drops dead.

I dreamed that you bewitched me into bed
And sung me moon-struck, kissed me quite insane.
(I think I made you up inside my head.)

God topples from the sky, hell's fires fade:
Exit Seraphim and Satan's men:
I shut my eyes and all the world drops dead.

I fancied you'd return the way you said.
But I grow old and I forget your name.
(I think I made you up inside my head.)

I should have loved a thunderbird instead;
At least when spring comes they roar back again.
I shut my eyes and all the world drops dead.
(I think I made you up inside my head.)

HOW WE HEARD THE NAME

alan dugan

The river brought down
dead horses, dead men
and military debris,
indicative of war
or official acts upstream,
but it went by, it all
goes by, that is the thing
about the river. Then
a soldier on a log
went by. He seemed drunk
and we asked him Why
had he and this junk
come down to us so
from the past upstream.
"Friends," he said, "the great
Battle of Granicus
has just been won
by all of the Greeks except
the Lacedaemonians and
myself: this is a joke
between me and a man
named Alexander, whom
all of you ba-bas
will hear of as a god."

THE GLADIATOR

kevin prufer » track 15 read by the poet

When I died

When my blood feathered away and I stared blankly and sideways

into the grass. When the grass ceased

against my cheek, I could not help

but remember the gladiator who, in falling, never groans,

who, ordered to accept it,

does not contract his neck for the final blow.

And the hillside grew quiet. The bombers passed

withering the trees and the city with flame. The empire

fell. My empire, like a blood drop into the grass.

It is of little consequence to the observer

if the gladiator falls forward into the dirt. He is of a mind, merely,

to do as he is told. He will not see the emperor's thumbs.

His city fell to its knees and burned, rolled on its side,

but he won't think of it. Those who once cheered for him

are cheering still. The airplanes

flew over the hill and I, crouched in the grass, was terrified

but did not look up, did not complain

when a last bomb startled me away.

WORTH

marilyn nelson » track 16 read by the poet

For Ruben Ahoueya

Today in America people were bought and sold:
five hundred for a "likely Negro wench."
If someone at auction is worth her weight in gold,
how much would she be worth by pound? By ounce?
If I owned an unimaginable quantity of wealth,
could I buy an iota of myself?
How would I know which part belonged to me?
If I owned part, could I set my part free?
It must be worth something—maybe a lot—
that my great-grandfather, they say, killed a lion.
They say he was black, with muscles as hard as iron,
that he wore a necklace of the claws of the lion he'd fought.
How much do I hear, for his majesty in my blood?
I auction myself. And I make the highest bid.

I AM A BLACK

gwendolyn brooks

According to my Teachers,
I am now an African-American.

They call me out of my name.

BLACK is an open umbrella.
I am a Black and A Black forever.

I am one of The Blacks.

We are Here, we are There.
We occur in Brazil, in Nigeria, Ghana,
in Botswana, Tanzania, in Kenya,
in Russia, Australia, in Haiti, Soweto,
in Grenada, in Cuba, in Panama, Libya,
in England and Italy, France.

We are graces in any places.
I am Black and A Black
forever.

I am other than Hyphenation.

I say, proudly, MY PEOPLE!
I say, proudly, OUR PEOPLE!

Our People do not disdain to eat yams or melons or grits
or to put peanut butter in stew.

I am Kojo. In West Afrika Kojo
mean Unconquerable. My parents
named me the seventh day from my birth
In Black spirit, Black faith, Black communion.
I am Kojo. I am A Black.
And I Capitalize my name.

Do not call me out of my name.

LOST SISTER

cathy song » track 17 read by the poet

1

In China,
Even the peasants
named their first daughters
Jade—
the stone that in the far fields
could moisten the dry season,
could make men move mountains
for the healing green of the inner hills
glistening like slices of winter melon.

And the daughters were grateful:
They never left home.
To move freely was a luxury
stolen from them at birth.
Instead, they gathered patience,
learning to walk in shoes
the size of teacups,
without breaking—
the arc of their movements
as dormant as the rooted willow,
as redundant as the farmyard hens.
But they travelled far
in surviving,
learning to stretch the family rice,
to quiet the demons,
the noisy stomachs.

2

There is a sister
across the ocean,
who relinquished her name,
diluting jade green
with the blue of the Pacific.
Rising with a tide of locusts,
she swarmed with others
to inundate another shore.
In America,
there are many roads
and women can stride along with men.

But in another wilderness,
the possibilities,
the loneliness,
can strangulate like jungle vines.
The meager provisions and sentiments
of once belonging—
fermented roots, Mah-Jongg tiles and firecrackers—
set but a flimsy household
in a forest of nightless cities.
A giant snake rattles above,
spewing black clouds into your kitchen.
Dough-faced landlords
slip in and out of your keyholes,
making claims you don't understand,
tapping into your communication systems
of laundry lines and restaurant chains.

You find you need China:
your one fragile identification,
a jade link
handcuffed to your wrist.
You remember your mother
who walked for centuries,
footless—
and like her,
you have left no footprints,
but only because
there is an ocean in between,
the unremitting space of your rebellion.

FLASH CARDS

rita dove » **track 18** read by the poet

In math I was the whiz kid, keeper
of oranges and apples. *What you don't understand,
master,* my father said; the faster
I answered, the faster they came.

I could see one bud on the teacher's geranium,
one clear bee sputtering at the wet pane.
The tulip trees always dragged after heavy rain
so I tucked my head as my boots slapped home.

My father put up his feet after work
and relaxed with a highball and *The Life of Lincoln.*
After supper we drilled and I climbed the dark

before sleep, before a thin voice hissed
numbers as I spun on a wheel. I had to guess.
Ten, I kept saying, *I'm only ten.*

ARITHMETIC

carl sandburg

Arithmetic is where numbers fly like pigeons in and out of your
head.

Arithmetic tells you how many you lose or win if you know how
many you had before you lost or won.

Arithmetic is seven eleven all good children go to heaven—or five
six bundle of sticks.

Arithmetic is numbers you squeeze from your head to your hand
to your pencil to your paper till you get the answer.

Arithmetic is where the answer is right and everything is nice and
you can look out of the window and see the blue sky—or the
answer is wrong and you have to start all over and try again
and see how it comes out this time.

If you take a number and double it and double it again and then
double it a few more times, the number gets bigger and bigger
and goes higher and higher and only arithmetic can tell you
what the number is when you decide to quit doubling.

Arithmetic is where you have to multiply—and you carry the
multiplication table in your head and hope you won't lose it.

If you have two animal crackers, one good and one bad, and you
eat one and a striped zebra with streaks all over him eats the
other, how many animal crackers will you have if somebody
offers you five six seven and you say No no no and you say
Nay nay nay and you say Nix nix nix?

If you ask your mother for one fried egg for breakfast and she
gives you two fried eggs and you eat both of them, who is
better in arithmetic, you or your mother?

DREAM VARIATIONS

langston hughes » track 19 read by the poet

To fling my arms wide
In some place of the sun,
To whirl and to dance
Till the white day is done.
Then rest at cool evening
Beneath a tall tree
While night comes on gently,
  Dark like me—
That is my dream!

To fling my arms wide
In the face of the sun,
Dance! Whirl! Whirl!
Till the quick day is done.
Rest at pale evening...
A tall, slim tree...
Night coming tenderly
  Black like me.

DREAMS

langston hughes

Hold fast to dreams
For if dreams die
Life is a broken-winged bird
That cannot fly.

Hold fast to dreams
For when dreams go
Life is a barren field
Frozen with snow.

BLACKBERRY-PICKING

seamus heaney

Late August, given heavy rain and sun
For a full week, the blackberries would ripen.
At first, just one, a glossy purple clot
Among others, red, green, hard as a knot.
You ate that first one and its flesh was sweet
Like thickened wine: summer's blood was in it
Leaving stains upon the tongue and lust for
Picking. Then red ones inked up and that hunger
Sent us out with milk cans, pea tins, jam-pots
Where briars scratched and wet grass bleached our boots.
Round hayfields, cornfields and potato-drills
We trekked and picked until the cans were full,
Until the tinkling bottom had been covered
With green ones, and on top big dark blobs burned
Like a plate of eyes. Our hands were peppered
With thorn pricks, our palms sticky as Bluebeard's.

We hoarded the fresh berries in the byre.
But when the bath was filled we found a fur,
A rat-grey fungus, glutting on our cache.
The juice was stinking too. Once off the bush
The fruit fermented, the sweet flesh would turn sour.
I always felt like crying. It wasn't fair
That all the lovely canfuls smelt of rot.
Each year I hoped they'd keep, knew they would not.

MANNERS
FOR A CHILD OF 1918

elizabeth bishop

My grandfather said to me
as we sat on the wagon seat,
"Be sure to remember to always
speak to everyone you meet."

We met a stranger on foot.
My grandfather's whip tapped his hat.
"Good day, sir. Good day. A fine day."
And I said it and bowed where I sat.

Then we overtook a boy we knew
with his big pet crow on his shoulder.
"Always offer everyone a ride;
don't forget that when you get older,"

my grandfather said. So Willy
climbed up with us, but the crow
gave a "Caw!" and flew off. I was worried.
How would he know where to go?

But he flew a little way at a time
from fence post to fence post, ahead;
and when Willy whistled he answered.
"A fine bird," my grandfather said,

"and he's well brought up. See, he answers
nicely when he's spoken to.
Man or beast, that's good manners.
Be sure that you both always do."

When automobiles went by,
the dust hid the people's faces,
but we shouted "Good day! Good day!
Fine day!" at the top of our voices.

When we came to Hustler Hill,
he said that the mare was tired,
so we all got down and walked,
as our good manners required.

MASCARA

elizabeth spires » track 20 read by the poet

For Ann

One eye swims into view, bright as a fish,
enlarged, and swiftly the eyelash lengthens,
grows, the eye pools to its own longing,
as you twirl the mascara wand and smile,
then frown, at what you see, shadowing
the eyebrow, the cheek's hollow, wishing
for what? I don't know. Over your shoulder,
I see my own face, unmasked, ten years apart
from you, an old moon looking at the new.
Then cheek to cheek, we stare for one
bright moment in the mirror, as close
as old injuries, forgotten but not entirely
forgiven, will allow. We share each other's
face, as sisters do. The mirror glows.

FROM
FOR A GIRL BECOMING

joy harjo » track 21 read by the poet

for Krista Rae Chico

Don't forget how you started your journey from that rainbow house,
How you traveled and will travel through the mountains and valleys
of human tests.
There are treacherous places along the way, but you can come to us.
There are lakes of tears shimmering sadly there, but you can come to us.
And valleys without horses or kindnesses, but you can come to us.
And angry, jealous gods and wayward humans who will hurt you,
but you can come to us.
You will fall, but you will get back up again, because you are one of us.

And as you travel with us remember this:
Give a drink of water to all who ask, whether they be plant, creature,
human or helpful spirit;
May you always have clean, fresh, water.

Feed your neighbors. Give kind words and assistance
to all you meet along the way. We are all related in this place.
May you be surrounded with the helpfulness of family and good friends.

Grieve with the grieving, share joy with the joyful.
May you build a strong path with beautiful and truthful language.

Clean your room.

May you always have a home: a refuge from storm, a gathering place
   for safety, for comfort.

Bury what needs to be buried.

Laugh easily at yourself.

May you always travel lightly and well.

Praise and give thanks for each small and large thing.

May you grow in knowledge, in compassion, in beauty.

Always within you is that day your spirit came to us

When rains came in from the Pacific to bless

They peered over the mountains in response to the singing of medicine plants

Who danced back and forth in shawls of mist

Your mother labored there, so young in earthly years.

And we who love you gather here,

Pollen blows throughout this desert house to bless

And horses run the land, hundreds of them for you,

And you are here to bless.

EVERY DAY IT IS ALWAYS THERE

rainy ortiz » **track 22** read by the poet

Every day it is always there
Whether in mind or body
Whether I want it to be or not—
Sometimes it's like being haunted
By a constant presence
Of sometimes happiness
Sometimes anger—
But it is always filled with love.
That love is my protector.
That protector is my mother.

DEAR MAMA (4)

wanda coleman » track 23 read by the poet

when did we become friends?
it happened so gradual i didn't notice
maybe i had to get my run out first
take a big bite of the honky world and choke on it
maybe that's what has to happen with some uppity
   youngsters
if it happens at all

and now
the thought stark and irrevocable
of being here without you
shakes me

beyond love, fear, regret or anger
into that realm children go
who want to care for/protect their parents
as if they could
and sometimes the lucky ones do

into the realm of making every moment
important
laughing as though laughter wards off death
each word given
received like spanish eight

treasure to bury within
against that shadow day
when it will be the only coin i possess
with which to buy peace of mind

A BOY IN A BED IN THE DARK

brad sachs

Born with a cleft palate,
My two-year-old brother,
Recovering from yet another surgery,
Toddled into our bedroom
Toppled a tower of blocks
That I had patiently built
And in a five-year-old's fury
I grabbed a fallen block
And winged it at him
Ripping open his carefully reconstructed lip.
The next hours were gruesomely compressed
Ending with a boy in a bed in the dark
Mute with fear
Staring out into the hallway with horror
As the pediatrician went in and out of the bathroom
With one vast blood-soaked towel after another
Shaking his head worriedly.
My brother's howls
And my parents' cooed comfort
Became the soundtrack to this milky movie
That plays
In my darkest theatre,
The one that I sidle past each night
With a shudder
And a throb in my fist

THE TALK

sharon olds

In the dark square wooden room at noon
the mother had a talk with her daughter.
The rudeness could not go on, the meanness
to her little brother, the selfishness.
The 8-year-old sat on the bed
in the corner of the room, her irises dark as
the last drops of something, her firm
face melting, reddening,
silver flashes in her eyes like distant
bodies of water glimpsed through woods.
She took it and took it and broke, crying out
I hate being a person! diving
into the mother
as if
into
a deep pond—and she cannot swim,
the child cannot swim.

A SMALL POEM

calvin forbes » track 24 read by the poet

shade is cool
that's what and why
he named his son

shade son of shine
a man might/can grow
to fit his name

a child can be a seed
that grows to shade
a seedy old man

a man can live up
to what he's bringing up
a man can be a child

a child can't be a man
this is why the son
had shine for his father

to learn why/what's going
down and coming up
to grow up until a grown up

FEARS OF THE EIGHTH GRADE

toi derricotte » track 25 read by the poet

When I ask what things they fear,
their arms raise like soldiers volunteering for battle:
Fear of going into a dark room, my murderer is waiting.
Fear of taking a shower, someone will stab me.
Fear of being kidnapped, raped.
Fear of dying in war.
When I ask how many fear this,
all the children raise their hands.

I think of this little box of consecrated land,
the bombs somewhere else,
the dead children in their mothers' arms,
women crying at the gates of the bamboo palace.

How thin the veneer!
The paper towels, napkins, toilet paper—everything
burned up in a day.

These children see the city after Armageddon.
The demons stand visible in the air
between their friends and talking.

WHEN I HAVE FEARS THAT I MAY CEASE TO BE

john keats

When I have fears that I may cease to be
Before my pen has glean'd my teeming brain,
Before high piled books, in charact'ry,
Hold like rich garners the full-ripen'd grain;
When I behold, upon the night's starr'd face,
Huge cloudy symbols of a high romance,
And think that I may never live to trace
Their shadows, with the magic hand of chance;
And when I feel, fair creature of an hour!
That I shall never look upon thee more,
Never have relish in the faery power
Of unreflecting love;—then on the shore
Of the wide world I stand alone, and think,
Till Love and Fame to nothingness do sink.

DEATH OF A SNOWMAN

vernon scannell

I was awake all night,
Big as a polar bear,
Strong and firm and white.
The tall black hat I wear
Was draped with ermine fur.
I felt so fit and well
Till the world began to stir
And the morning sun swell.
I was tired, began to yawn;
At noon in the humming sum
I caught a severe warm;
My nose began to run.
My hat grew black and fell,
Was followed by my grey head.
There was no funeral bell,
But by tea-time I was dead.

OATMEAL

galway kinnell

I eat oatmeal for breakfast.

I make it on the hot plate and put skimmed milk on it.

I eat it alone.

I am aware it is not good to eat oatmeal alone.

Its consistency is such that is better for your mental health if somebody
eats it with you.

That is why I often think up an imaginary companion to have breakfast with.

Possibly it is even worse to eat oatmeal with an imaginary companion.

Nevertheless, yesterday morning, I ate my oatmeal—porridge, as he called
it—with John Keats.

Keats said I was absolutely right to invite him: due to its glutinous texture,
gluey lumpishness, hint of slime, and unusual willingness to disintegrate,
oatmeal must never be eaten alone.

He said that in his opinion, however, it is perfectly OK to eat it with an
imaginary companion,

and that he himself had enjoyed memorable porridges with Edmund Spenser
and John Milton.

Even if eating oatmeal with an imaginary companion is not as wholesome as
Keats claims, still, you can learn something from it.

Yesterday morning, for instance, Keats told me about writing the "Ode to
a Nightingale."

He had a heck of a time finishing it—those were his words—"Oi'ad a 'eck of
a toime," he said, more or less, speaking through his porridge.

He wrote it quickly, on scraps of paper, which he then stuck in his pocket,
but when he got home he couldn't figure out the order of the stanzas, and he

and a friend spread the papers on a table, and they made some sense of
them, but he isn't sure to this day if they got it right.

An entire stanza may have slipped into the lining of his jacket through a
hole in his pocket.

He still wonders about the occasional sense of drift between stanzas,
and the way here and there a line will go into the configuration of a Moslem
at prayer, then raise itself up and peer about, and then lay itself down
slightly off the mark, causing the poem to move forward with God's
reckless wobble.

He said someone told him that later in life Wordsworth heard about the
scraps of paper on the table, and tried shuffling some stanzas of his own,
but only made matters worse.

I would not have known any of this but for my reluctance to eat
oatmeal alone.

When breakfast was over, John recited "To Autumn."

He recited it slowly, with much feeling, and he articulated the words
lovingly, and his odd accent sounded sweet.

He didn't offer the story of writing "To Autumn," I doubt if there is much
of one.

But he did say the sight of a just-harvested oat field got him started on it,
and two of the lines, "For Summer has o'er-brimmed their clammy cells"
and "Thou watchest the last oozings hours by hours," came to him while
eating oatmeal alone.

I can see him—drawing a spoon through the stuff, gazing into the glimmering
furrows, muttering—and it occurs to me:

maybe there is no sublime; only the shining of the amnion's tatters.

For supper tonight I am going to have a baked potato left over from lunch.

I am aware that a leftover baked potato is damp, slippery, and simultaneously
gummy and crumbly,

and therefore I'm going to invite Patrick Kavanagh to join me.

EATING POETRY

mark strand

I

Eating Poetry

Ink runs from the corners of my mouth.
There is no happiness like mine.
I have been eating poetry.

The librarian does not believe what she sees.
Her eyes are sad
and she walks with her hands in her dress.

The poems are gone.
The light is dim.
The dogs are on the basement stairs and coming up.

Their eyeballs roll,
their blond legs burn like brush.
The poor librarian begins to stamp her feet and weep.

She does not understand.
When I get on my knees and lick her hand,
she screams.

I am a new man,
I snarl at her and bark,
I romp with joy in the bookish dark.

THE BAGEL

david ignatow

I stopped to pick up the bagel
rolling away in the wind,
annoyed with myself
for having dropped it
as if it were a portent.
Faster and faster it rolled,
with me running after it
bent low, gritting my teeth,
and I found myself doubled over
and rolling down the street
head over heels, one complete somersault
after another like a bagel
and strangely happy with myself.

HOPE IS THE THING WITH FEATHERS

emily dickinson » track 26 read by Elise Paschen

Hope is the thing with feathers
That perches in the soul,
And sings the tune without the words,
And never stops at all,

And sweetest in the gale is heard;
And sore must be the storm
That could abash the little bird
That kept so many warm.

I've heard it in the chillest land
And on the strangest sea;
Yet, never, in extremity,
It asked a crumb of me.

IF I CAN STOP ONE HEART FROM BREAKING

emily dickinson

If I can stop one heart from breaking,

I shall not live in vain;

If I can ease one life the aching,

Or cool one pain,

Or help one fainting robin

Unto his nest again,

I shall not live in vain.

THE DUKE'S CASTLE

john fuller

I dreamed of the castle. Flying about
Were loosened trees, and I in my shirt
Saw sheets of water begin to shout.
I dreamed of the castle flying about:
Its turrets put the owls in doubt.
In my singing shirt I flew unhurt.
I dreamed of the castle. Flying about
Were loosened trees and I in my shirt.

Silence of chimneys ordered the air.
You were not there though bells were appealing.
I saw my childhood in rooftops where
Silence of chimneys ordered the air
To stand quite still and let me stare.
A tower of smoke became a feeling.
Silence of chimneys ordered the air.
You were not there, though. Bells were appealing.

The castle said nothing. Someone was calling
"Come back, come back." I cried in my sleep
And asked the castle to stop me from falling.
The castle said nothing. Someone was calling.
The stones looked ready for my sprawling.
I shouted: "What *is* there for me to keep?"
The castle said: "Nothing." Someone was calling.
"Come back, come back," I cried in my sleep.

OZYMANDIAS

percy bysshe shelley

I met a traveler from an antique land
Who said: Two vast and trunkless legs of stone
Stand in the desert...Near them, on the sand,
Half sunk, a shattered visage lies, whose frown,
And wrinkled lip, and sneer of cold command,
Tell that its sculptor well those passions read
Which yet survive, stamped on these lifeless things,
The hand that mocked them, and the heart that fed:
And on the pedestal these words appear:
"My name is Ozymandias, king of kings:
Look on my works, ye Mighty, and despair"
Nothing beside remains. Round the decay
Of that colossal wreck, boundless and bare
The lone and level sands stretch far away.

THE SACRED

stephen dunn » track 27 read by the poet

After the teacher asked if anyone had
    a sacred place
and the students fidgeted and shrunk

in their chairs, the most serious of them all
    said it was his car,
being in it alone, his tape deck playing

things he'd chosen, and others knew the truth
    had been spoken
and began speaking about their rooms,

their hiding places, but the car kept coming
    up, the car in motion,
music filling it, and sometimes one other person

who understood the bright altar of the dashboard
    and how far away
a car could take him from the need

to speak, or to answer, the key
    in having a key
and putting it in, and going.

THE ROAD NOT TAKEN

robert frost

Two roads diverged in a yellow wood, A
And sorry I could not travel both B
And be one traveler, long I stood A
And looked down one as far as I could A
To where it bent in the undergrowth; B

Then took the other, as just as fair, C
And having perhaps the better claim, A
Because it was grassy and wanted wear; C
Though as for that the passing there C
Had worn them really about the same, d

And both that morning equally lay e
In leaves no step had trodden black. f
Oh, I kept the first for another day! e
Yet knowing how way leads on to way, e
I doubted if I should ever come back. f

I shall be telling this with a sigh g
Somewhere ages and ages hence: h
Two roads diverged in a wood, and I— g
I took the one less traveled by, g
And that has made all the difference. h

PROWESS

samuel menashe

My nose shapes
Its own space
Opening a way
For my face.

WHAT WE MIGHT BE, WHAT WE ARE

x. j. kennedy » track 28 read by the poet

If you were a scoop of vanilla
And I were the cone where you sat,
If you were a slowly pitched baseball
And I were the swing of the bat,

If you were a shiny new fishhook
And I were a bucket of worms,
If we were a pin and pincushion,
We might be on intimate terms.

If you were a plate of spaghetti,
And I were your piping hot sauce,
We'd not even need to write e-mail
To put our affection across

But you're just a piece of red ribbon
In the beard of a Balinese goat,
And I'm a New Jersey mosquito.
I guess we'll stay slightly remote.

SIDEMAN

paul muldoon » track 29 performed by Rackett

I'll be the Road Runner
to your Wile E. Coyote
I'll take you in my stride
I'll be a Sancho Panza
to your Don Quixote
your ever faithful guide

I'll stand by you in the lists
with our market strategists
I'll be your sideman, baby,
I'll be by your side

I'll be a Keith Richards
to your Mick Jagger
before he let things slide
I'll be Sears to your Roebuck
before he took the headstaggers
and opened nationwide

I'll support you at Wembley
I may require some assembly
but I'll be your sideman, baby,
I'll be by your side

I'll be McCartney to your Lennon
Lenin to your Marx
Jerry to your Ben &
Lewis to your Clark
Burke to your Hare
James Bond to your Q
Booboo to your Yogi Bear
Tigger to your Pooh
Trigger to your Roy Rogers
Roy to your Siegfried
Fagin to your Artful Dodger
I guess I'll let you take the lead

I'll be a chingachgook
to your leatherstocking
a blaze of fur and hide
our shares consolidated
our directorates interlocking
I'll be along for the ride

I'll be at Ticonderoga
I'll be there for you at yoga
I'll be your sideman, baby,
I'll be by your side

XVIII. OH, WHEN I WAS IN LOVE WITH YOU

a. e. housman

Oh, when I was in love with you,
  Then I was clean and brave,
And miles around the wonder grew
  How well did I behave.

And now the fancy passes by,
  And nothing will remain,
And miles around they'll say that I
  Am quite myself again.

SOMETIMES WITH ONE I LOVE

walt whitman

Sometimes with one I love I fill myself with rage for
    fear I effuse unreturn'd love,
But now I think there is no unreturn'd love, the pay is
    certain one way or another,
(I loved a certain person ardently and my love was
    not return'd,
Yet out of that I have written these songs.)

IN THE DESERT

stephen crane

In the desert
I saw a creature, naked, bestial,
Who, squatting upon the ground,
Held his heart in his hands,
And ate of it.
I said, "Is it good, friend?"
"It is bitter—bitter," he answered,
"But I like it
Because it is bitter,
And because it is my heart."

ANNABEL LEE

edgar allan poe

It was many and many a year ago,
    In a kingdom by the sea,
That a maiden there lived whom you may know
    By the name of Annabel Lee;
And this maiden she lived with no other thought
    Than to love and be loved by me.

She was a child and *I* was a child,
    In this kingdom by the sea,
But we loved with a love that was more than love—
    I and my Annabel Lee—
With a love that the wingéd seraphs of Heaven
    Coveted her and me.

And this was the reason that, long ago,
    In this kingdom by the sea,
A wind blew out of a cloud by night
    Chilling my Annabel Lee;
So that her highborn kinsmen came
    And bore her away from me,
To shut her up in a sepulchre
    In this kingdom by the sea.

The angels, not half so happy in Heaven,
    Went envying her and me:
Yes! that was the reason (as all men know,
    In this kingdom by the sea)
That the wind came out of the cloud, chilling
    And killing my Annabel Lee.

But our love it was stronger by far than the love
    Of those who were older than we—
    Of many far wiser than we—
And neither the angels in Heaven above
    Nor the demons down under the sea,
Can ever dissever my soul from the soul
    Of the beautiful Annabel Lee:

For the moon never beams without bringing me dreams
    Of the beautiful Annabel Lee;
And the stars never rise but I see the bright eyes
    Of the beautiful Annabel Lee;
And so, all the night-tide, I lie down by the side
Of my darling, my darling, my life and my bride,
    In her sepulchre there by the sea—
    In her tomb by the side of the sea.

THE SUMMER OF BLACK WIDOWS

sherman alexie

The spiders appeared suddenly
after that summer rainstorm.

Some people still insist the spiders fell with the rain
while others believe the spiders grew from the damp soil like weeds
   with eight thin roots.

The elders knew the spiders
carried stories in their stomachs.

We tucked our pants into our boots when we walked through fields
   of fallow stories.
An Indian girl opened the closet door and a story fell into her hair.
We lived in the shadow of a story trapped in the ceiling lamp.
The husk of a story museumed on the windowsill.
Before sleep, we shook our blankets and stories fell to the floor.
A story floated in a glass of water left on the kitchen table.
We opened doors slowly and listened for stories.
The stories rose on hind legs and offered their red bellies to the most
   beautiful Indians.
Stories in our cereal boxes.

Stories in our firewood.
Stories in the pocket of our coats.
We captured stories and offered them to the ants, who carried the
  stories back to their queen.
A dozen stories per acre.
We poisoned the stories and gathered their remains with broom
  and pan.

The spiders disappeared suddenly
after that summer lightning storm.

Some people insist the spiders were burned to ash
while others believe the spiders climbed the lightning bolts and
  became a new constellation.

The elders knew the spiders
Had left behind bundles of stories.

Up in the corners of our old houses
we still find those small, white bundles
and nothing, neither fire
nor water, neither rock nor wind,
can bring them down.

PERMANENTLY

kenneth koch

One day the Nouns were clustered in the street.
An Adjective walked by, with her dark beauty.
The Nouns were struck, moved, changed.
The next day a Verb drove up, and created the Sentence.

Each Sentence says one thing—for example, "Although it was a dark rainy
   day when the Adjective walked by, I shall remember the pure and sweet
   expression on her face until the day I perish from the green, effective earth."
Or, "Will you please close the window, Andrew?"
Or, for example, "Thank you, the pink pot of flowers on the window sill
   has changed color recently to a light yellow, due to the heat from the
   boiler factory which exists nearby."

In the springtime the Sentences and the Nouns lay silently on the grass.
A lonely Conjunction here and there would call, "And! But!"
But the Adjective did not emerge.

As the Adjective is lost in the sentence,
So I am lost in your eyes, ears, nose, and throat—
You have enchanted me with a single kiss
Which can never be undone
Until the destruction of language.

A DOG ON HIS MASTER

billy collins » track 30 read by the poet

As young as I look,
I am growing older faster than he,
seven to one
is the ratio they tend to say.

Whatever the number,
I will pass him one day
and take the lead
the way I do on our walks in the woods.

And if this ever manages
to cross his mind,
it would be the sweetest
shadow I have ever cast on snow or grass.

MOWING

midge goldberg

You know those chores you always have to do,
like mowing grass: I grumble, go outside—
a lawn this size will take an hour or two
at least—put on my Red Sox hat and ride
around designing circles, lines, a border.
I move from shade to sunshine, deftly steering,
looking purposeful and bringing order
so neat and sure—and sure of disappearing.
With all this sun, I know that what I'm doing
won't last, won't keep a week; I ride about
to find the pleasure in the not pursuing,
to learn beyond the shadow of a doubt
the patterns that I long to bring to pass
get mown and overgrown like summer grass.

sonnet poem

SEAL

william jay smith

See how he dives
From the rocks with a zoom!
See how he darts
Through his watery room
Past crabs and eels
And green seaweed,
Past fluffs of sandy
Minnow feed!
See how he swims
With a swerve and a twist,
A flip of the flipper,
A flick of the wrist!
Quicksilver-quick,
Softer than spray,
Down he plunges
And sweeps away;
Before you can think,
Before you can utter
Words like "Dill pickle"
Or "Apple butter,"
Back up he swims
Past sting-ray and shark,
Out with a zoom,
A whoop, a bark;
Before you can say
Whatever you wish,
He plops at your side
With a mouthful of fish!

SEAHORSES

brad leithauser

Kin to all kinds
Of fancied hybrids—minotaur
　　And wyvern, cockatrice,
Kyrin and griffin—this
Monkey-tailed, dragon-chested
　　Prankish twist of whimsy
Outshines that whole composited
Menagerie, for this sequined
　　Equine wonder, howsoever
　　Improbably,

　　Quite palpably
Exists! Within his moted
　　Medium, tail loosely laced
Round the living hitching post
Of a coral twig, he feeds at leisure
　　As befits a mild, compromising
Creature with no arms of defence
Save that of, in his knobby
　　Sparsity, appearing
　　Unappetizing.

Like that chess piece
He so resembles, he glides
        With a forking, oblique
Efficiency, the winglike
Fins behind his ears aflutter;
        And like that lone
Unmastered steed to whom
The word-weary everywhere
        Look for replenishment—
            That is to say, our own

            Like-winged, light-winged
Pegasus—he can be taken
        As an embodiment
Of the obscure fount
And unaccountable buoyancy
        Of artistic inspiration.
Yet defined by neither,
Finally, by nothing afloat
        On the long, circulating
            Seas of creation,

        Is this mailed male
Who bears in his own brood pouch
        A female's transferred conceptions,
And seems to move (those fins
By turns transparent) through
        Telekinetic promptings, while his
Turreted, nonsynchronous
Eyes are taking in two
        Views at once. How appropriate
            That gaze of his is—

For he conveys
A sense of living at least two
Simultaneous lives, of always
Having a mucilaginous
If metaphorical foot
Planted in a neighbouring, renum-
bered dimension, one whose
Dim-sensed presence releases our
Ineffable but hopeful
Yearnings for some

Further release.
In his otherworldliness
He heartens us....If there's to be
Any egress for you and me
From the straitening domain
Of the plausible, what course
More likely than astride the plated
Shoulders of this shimmering
Upright swimmer, this
Waterbound winged horse?

SO FAR

naomi shihab nye » track 31 read by the poet

notices flutter
    from telephone poles
      until they fade

OUR SWEET TABBY   AFRAID OF EVERYTHING
BIG GRAY CAT   HE IS OUR ONLY CHILD
SIBERIAN HUSKY   NEEDS HIS MEDICINE
FEMALE SCHNAUZER   WE ARE SICK WITH WORRY

    all night I imagine their feet
     tapping up the sidewalk
   under the blooming crepe myrtle
    and the swoon of jasmine
      into the secret hedges
        into the dark cool caves
     of the banana-palm grove
    and we cannot catch them
    or know what they are thinking
   when they go so far from home

OUR BELOVED TURTLE   RED DOT ON FOREHEAD
VEGETARIAN   NAME OF KALI

please please please
  if you see them
call me call me call me

THE GERM

ogden nash

A mighty creature is the germ,
Though smaller than the pachyderm.
His customary dwelling place
Is deep within the human race.
His childish pride he often pleases
By giving people strange diseases.
Do you, my poppet, feel infirm?
You probably contain a germ.

BASEBALL

bill zavatsky » track 32 read by the poet

We were only farm team
not "good enough" to
make big Little League
with its classic uniforms,
deep lettered hats.
But our coach said
we *were* just as good,
maybe better,
so we played
the Little League champs
in our stenciled tee shirts
and soft purple caps
when the season was over.

What happened that afternoon
I can't remember—
whether we won or tied.
But in my mind I lean back
to a pop-up hanging
in sunny sky,
stopped,
nailed to the blue,
losing itself in a cloud
over second base
where I stood waiting.

Ray Michaud, who knew,
my up-and-down career
as a local player,
my moments of graceful genius,
my unpredictable ineptness,
screamed arrows at me
from the dugout
where he waited to bat:
"He's gonna drop it! He
don't know how to catch,
you watch it drop!"

The ball kept climbing
higher, a black dot,
no rules of gravity, no
brakes, a period searching
for a sentence, and the sentence read:
"You're no good, Bill.
You won't catch this one now;
You know you never will."

I watched myself looking up
and felt my body rust, falling
in pieces to the ground,
a baby trying to stand up,
an ant in the shadow of a house.

I wasn't there—
had never been born,
would stand there forever,
a statue squinting upward,
pointed out, laughed at
for a thousand years
teammates dead, forgotten,
bones of anyone who played baseball
forgotten
baseball forgotten, played no more,
played by robots on electric fields
who never missed
or cried in their own sweat.

I'm a lot older now.
The game was over
a million years ago.
All I remember
of that afternoon
when the ball
came down
is that
I caught it

POETRY SLALOM

mary jo salter

Much less
the slam
than the slalom
gives me a thrill:
that solemn, no-fuss
Olympian skill
in skirting flag after flag
of the bloody obvious;
the fractional
lag,
while speeding downhill,
at the key
moment,
in a sort of whole-
body trill:
the note repeated,
but elaborated,
more touching and more
elevated
for seeming the thing
to be evaded.

HOW I DISCOVERED POETRY

marilyn nelson » track 33 read by the poet

It was like soul-kissing, the way the words
filled my mouth as Mrs. Purdy read from her desk.
All the other kids zoned an hour ahead to 3:15,
but Mrs. Purdy and I wandered lonely as clouds borne
by a breeze off Mount Parnassus. She must have seen
the darkest eyes in the room brim: The next day
she gave me a poem she'd chosen especially for me
to read to the all except for me white class.
She smiled when she told me to read it, smiled harder,
said oh yes I could. She smiled harder and harder
until I stood and opened my mouth to banjo playing
darkies, pickaninnies, disses and dats. When I finished
my classmates stared at the floor. We walked silent
to the buses, awed by the power of words.

USED BOOK SHOP

x. j. kennedy » track 34 read by the poet

Stashed in attics,
stuck in cellars,
forgotten books
once big best-sellers

now hopefully sit
where folks, like cows
in grassy meadows,
stand and browse.

In a yellowed old history
of Jesse James
two earlier owners
had scrawled their names.

I even found
a book my dad
when he was in high school
had once had,

and a book I found—
this is really odd—
was twice as much fun
as my new iPod.

I always get hooked
in this dusty shop.
Like eating popcorn,
it's hard to stop.

THE SURVIVOR

marilyn chin » track 35 read by the poet

Don't tap your chopsticks against your bowl.
Don't throw your teacup against the wall in anger.
Don't suck on your long black braid and weep.
Don't tarry around the big red sign that says "danger!"
*

That you have bloomed this way and not that,
that your skin is yellow, not white, not black,
that you were born not a boy-child but a girl,
that this world will be forever puce-pink are just as well.

Remember, the survivor is not the strongest or most clever;
merely, the survivor is almost always the youngest.
And you shall have to relinquish that title before long.

NEW CLOTHES

kay ryan » **tracks 36** & **37** read by the poet

The emperor who
was tricked by the tailors
is familiar to you.

But the tailors
keep on changing
what they do
to make money.

(*Tailor* means
to make something
fit somebody.)

Be guaranteed
that they will discover
your pride.

You will cast aside
something you cherish
when the tailors whisper,
"Only you could wear this."

It is almost never clothes
such as the emperor bought

but it is always something close
to something you've got.

MEDIATION

kim stafford

At the dinner table, before the thrown
plate, but after the bitter claim,
in the one beat of silence
before the parents declare war

their child, who had been temporarily
invisible, but who had from school
a catechism, speaks: "Would you like me
to help solve the conflict?" Silence.

They can't look at each other. A glance
would sear the soul. A wall of fire seethes,
Maginot line through the butter plate,
split salt from pepper, him from her. Silence.

So the child speaks: "Three rules, then:
One—you have to let each other finish.
Two—you have to tell the truth. Three—
you have to want to solve the conflict.

If you say yes, we will solve it.
I love you. What do you say?"

A FABLE

louise glück

Two women with
the same claim
came to the feet of
the wise king. Two women,
but only one baby.
The king knew
someone was lying.
What he said was
Let the child be
cut in half; that way
no one will go
empty-handed. He
drew his sword.
Then, of the two
women, one
renounced her share:
this was
the sign, the lesson.
Suppose
you saw your mother
torn between two daughters:
what could you do
to save her but be
willing to destroy
yourself—she would know
who was the rightful child,
the one who couldn't bear
to divide the mother.

HOUSES

nancy willard » track 38 read by the poet

My father's house was made of sky.
His bookcases stood twelve feet high.
The snowy owl my father tamed,
the stones he showed me, stars he named,
agate, quartz, the Milky Way—
"It's good to know their names," he'd say,
"so when I'm gone and you are grown,
in any world you'll feel at home."

My mother's house was made of talk,
words that could rouse a flea to flight
or make a stone stand up and walk.
Words filled the kitchen day and night.
Grandpa knew all the Psalms by heart.
My mother's sisters knew the art
of telling tales, and lies so new
all those who heard them called them true.

My house is quieter than theirs.
My promises are frail as foam.
I still forget to say my prayers.
Between the lines I plucked this poem.
Look up. To the discerning eye,
my house stands open to the sky.

SNOWMEN

agha shahid ali

My ancestor, a man
of Himalayan snow,
came to Kashmir from Samarkand,
carrying a bag
of whale bones:
heirlooms from sea funerals.
His skeleton
carved from glaciers, his breath
arctic,
he froze women in his embrace.
His wife thawed into stony water,
her old age a clear
evaporation.

This heirloom,
his skeleton under my skin, passed
from son to grandson,
generations of snowmen on my back.
They tap every year on my window,
their voices hushed to ice.

No, they won't let me out of winter,
and I've promised myself,
even if I'm the last snowman,
that I'll ride into spring
on their melting shoulders.

THE FLORAL APRON

marilyn chin » track 39 read by the poet

The woman wore a floral apron around her neck,
that woman from my mother's village
with a sharp cleaver in her hand.
She said, "What shall we cook tonight?
Perhaps these six tiny squid
lined up so perfectly on the block?"

She wiped her hand on the apron,
pierced the blade into the first.
There was no resistance,
no blood, only cartilage
soft as a child's nose. A last
iota of ink made us wince.

Suddenly, the aroma of ginger and scallion fogged our senses,
and we absolved her for that moment's barbarism.
Then, she, an elder of the tribe,
without formal headdress, without elegance,
deigned to teach the younger
about the Asian plight.

And although we have traveled far
we would never forget that primal lesson
—on patience, courage, forbearance,
on how to love squid despite squid,
how to honor the village, the tribe,
that floral apron.

ABUELITO WHO

sandra cisneros

Abuelito who throws coins like rain
and asks who loves him
who is dough and feathers
who is a watch and glass of water
whose hair is made of fur
is too sad to come downstairs today
who tells me in Spanish you are my diamond
who tells me in English you are my sky
whose little eyes are string
can't come out to play
sleeps in his little room all night and day
who used to laugh like the letter k
is sick
is a doorknob tied to a sour stick
is tired, shut the door
doesn't live here anymore
is hiding underneath the bed
who talks to me inside my head
is blankets and spoons and big brown shoes
who snores up and down up and down up and down again
is the rain on the room that falls like coins
asking who loves him
who loves him who?

LEGACIES

nikki giovanni

her grandmother called her from the playground
  "yes, ma'am"
  "i want chu to learn how to make rolls" said
  the old
woman proudly
but the little girl didn't want
to learn how because she knew
even if she couldn't say it that
that would mean when the old one died she would
be less
dependent on her spirit so
she said
  "i don't want to know how to make no rolls"
with her lips poked out
and the old woman wiped her hands on
her apron saying "lord
  these children"
and neither of them ever
said what they meant
and i guess nobody ever does

INSTEAD OF HER OWN

molly peacock » tracks 40 & 41 read by the poet

Instead of her own, my grandmother washed my hair.
The porcelain was cold at the back of my neck,
my fragile neck. Altogether it was cold there.

She did it so my hair would smell sweet.
What else is like the moist mouse straw
of a girl's head? Why, the feeling of complete

peace the smell brings to a room whose window
off oily Lake Erie is rimmed with snow.
Knuckles rasping at young temples know,

in the involuntary way a body knows,
that as old is, so young grows. Completion
drives us: substitution is our mission.

Thin little head below thin little head grown old.
Water almost warm in a room almost cold.

TIA CHUCHA

luis j. rodriguez

Every few years Tia Chucha would visit the family
in a tornado of song and open us up
as if we were an overripe avocado.
She was a dumpy, black-haired
creature of upheaval who often came unannounced
with a bag of presents, including homemade
perfumes and colognes that smelled something like
rotting fish on a hot day at the tuna cannery.

They said she was crazy. Oh sure, she once ran out naked
to catch the postman with a letter that didn't belong to us.
I mean, she had this annoying habit of boarding city buses
and singing at the top of her voice—one bus driver
even refused to go on until she got off.

But crazy?

To me, she was the wisp of the wind's freedom,
a music-maker who once tried to teach me guitar
but ended up singing and singing,
me listening, and her singing
until I put the instrument down
and watched the clock click the lesson time away.

I didn't learn guitar, but I learned something
about her craving for the new, the unbroken,
so she could break it. Periodically she banished herself
from the family—and was the better for it.

I secretly admired Tia Chucha.
She was always quick with a story,
another "Pepito" joke or a hand-written lyric
that she would produce regardless of the occasion.

She was a despot of desire,
uncontainable as a splash of water
on a varnished table.

I wanted to remove the layers
of unnatural seeing,
the way Tia Chucha beheld
the world, with first eyes,
like an infant who can discern
the elixir within milk.

I wanted to be one of the prizes
she stuffed into her rumpled bag.

THE ADVERSARY

phyllis mcginley

A mother's hardest to forgive.
Life is the fruit she longs to hand you,
Ripe on a plate. And while you live,
Relentlessly she understands you.

WHAT YOUR MOTHER TELLS YOU NOW

mitsuye yamada

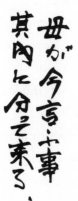

haha ga ima yu-koto
sono uchi ni
wakatte kuru

What your mother tells you
    now
in time
you will come to know.

33

philip schultz » **track 42** read by the poet

My bar mitzvah is going to be in The Grand Ballroom
of the Sheraton Hotel. Mother says: We live behind a junkyard
and can't afford cement in our basement but he's throwing
the biggest party since Moses heard voices. This is *our* opportunity
to show everyone we're alive and kicking, Father yells, anyone
can rent a back room. But why pay ten years for one night,
she yells back. To have a night to remember, he says, she thinks
too small, debt is how you establish credit, the more the better,
that's why he keeps buying new machines, doesn't own insurance
or belong to a temple—he wants to owe everyone, even God.
All I want is a bowling party, for it all to be over with...at night
Mother eats tuna fish out of a can, with a spoon, sighing...

49

philip schultz » **track 43** read by the poet

"Since I was a boy in Krakow a bar mitzvah is my
favorite ceremony," Rabbi Friedlander says in front
of the Torah Scroll, as Mother smiles from the balcony,
along with Moses, King David and Saul..."My father
David, sister Rebecca and brother William were all
still alive before the pogrom...now each year I awaken
to manhood to be tested again, as everything is a test
of God's love, even looking into the mirror, the boy
peeking through my old man's eyes, still frightened...
therefore"—now he looks at me—"I am happy to
welcome up to the Book to give his Aliyah blessing..."
Legless, I walk to the bimah where the sextons step
aside and the rabbi whispers, "Good luck, my boy,"
and, my eyes shut to not see all the faces, I listen
for the words to come out of my mouth, like breath...

WHAT ARE HEAVY?

christina rossetti

What are heavy? Sea-sand and sorrow;
What are brief? Today and Tomorrow;
What are frail? Spring blossoms and youth;
What are deep? The ocean and truth.

THE WIND

sara teasdale

A wind is blowing over my soul,
I hear it cry the whole night thro'—
Is there no peace for me on earth
Except with you?

Alas, the wind has made me wise,
Over my naked soul it blew,—
There is no peace for me on earth
Even with you.

ACQUAINTED WITH THE NIGHT

robert frost » track 44 read by the poet

I have been one acquainted with the night.
I have walked out in rain—and back in rain.
I have outwalked the furthest city light.

I have looked down the saddest city lane.
I have passed by the watchman on his beat
And dropped my eyes, unwilling to explain.

I have stood still and stopped the sound of feet
When far away an interrupted cry
Came over houses from another street,

But not to call me back or say good-by;
And further still at an unearthly height,
One luminary clock against the sky

Proclaimed the time was neither wrong nor right.
I have been one acquainted with the night.

sonnet

WHEN YOU ARE OLD

w. b. yeats » track 45 read by Elise Paschen

When you are old and grey and full of sleep,
And nodding by the fire, take down this book,
And slowly read, and dream of the soft look
Your eyes had once, and of their shadows deep;

How many loved your moments of glad grace,
And loved your beauty with love false or true,
But one man loved the pilgrim soul in you,
And loved the sorrows of your changing face;

And bending down beside the glowing bars,
Murmur, a little sadly, how Love fled
And paced upon the mountains overhead
And hid his face amid a crowd of stars.

rainer maria rilke

Nobody can counsel and help you, nobody. There is only one single way. Go into yourself. Search for the reason that bids you write; find out whether it is spreading out its roots in the deepest places of your heart, acknowledge to yourself whether you would have to die if it were denied you to write. This above all—ask yourself in the stillest hour of your night: *must* I write? Delve into yourself for a deep answer. And if this should be affirmative, if you may meet this earnest question with a strong and simple *"I must,"* then build your life according to this necessity; your life even into its most indifferent and slightest hour must be a sign of this urge and a testimony to it. Then draw near to Nature. Then try, like some first human being, to say what you see and experience and love and lose.

rainer maria rilke

Live a while in these books, learn from them what seems to you worth learning, but above all love them. This love will be repaid you a thousand and a thousand times, and however your life may turn,—it will, I am certain of it, run through the fabric of your growth as one of the most important threads among all the threads of your experiences, disappointments and joys.

HERE YET BE DRAGONS

lucille clifton

so many languages have fallen
off of the edge of the world
into the dragon's mouth. some

where there be monsters whose teeth
are sharp and sparkle with lost

people. lost poems. who
among us can imagine ourselves
unimagined? who

among us can speak with so fragile
tongue and remain proud?

SEDNA

kimiko hahn » track 46 read by the poet

Come to find out, Sedna,
is the Inuit woman,

whose father cast her from their kayak,
thus transforming her into the spirit of the sea—

but also the name of 2003 VB12,

a planet or something beyond Pluto.
It is the first body to be discovered

in the Oort Cloud, *a hypothetical region
of icy objects that become comets.*

But questions remain: how
can a region be hypothetical?

how can a scientist not know

what a planet is? how could a father
throw his daughter from a kayak

even if she did write poetry
that hurt his feelings?

I am not sorry.
He always said, *art comes first*.

But that is a murky region

for fathers and daughters—
what comes first.

And what my daughters wish to know is
did she drown for his sake

or to learn how depths betray?

THE WRITER

richard wilbur » **track 47** read by the poet

In her room at the prow of the house
Where light breaks, and the windows are tossed with linden,
My daughter is writing a story.

I pause in the stairwell, hearing
From her shut door a commotion of typewriter-keys
Like a chain hauled over a gunwale.

Young as she is, the stuff
Of her life is a great cargo, and some of it heavy:
I wish her a lucky passage.

But now it is she who pauses,
As if to reject my thought and its easy figure.
A stillness greatens, in which

The whole house seems to be thinking,
And then she is at it again with a bunched clamor
Of strokes, and again is silent.

I remember the dazed starling
Which was trapped in that very room, two years ago;
How we stole in, lifted a sash

And retreated, not to affright it;
And how for a helpless hour, through the crack of
   the door,
We watched the sleek, wild, dark

And iridescent creature
Batter against the brilliance, drop like a glove
To the hard floor, or the desk-top,

And wait then, humped and bloody,
For the wits to try it again; and how our spirits
Rose when, suddenly sure,

It lifted off from a chair-back,
Beating a smooth course for the right window
And clearing the sill of the world.

It is always a matter, my darling,
Of life or death, as I had forgotten. I wish
What I wished you before, but harder.

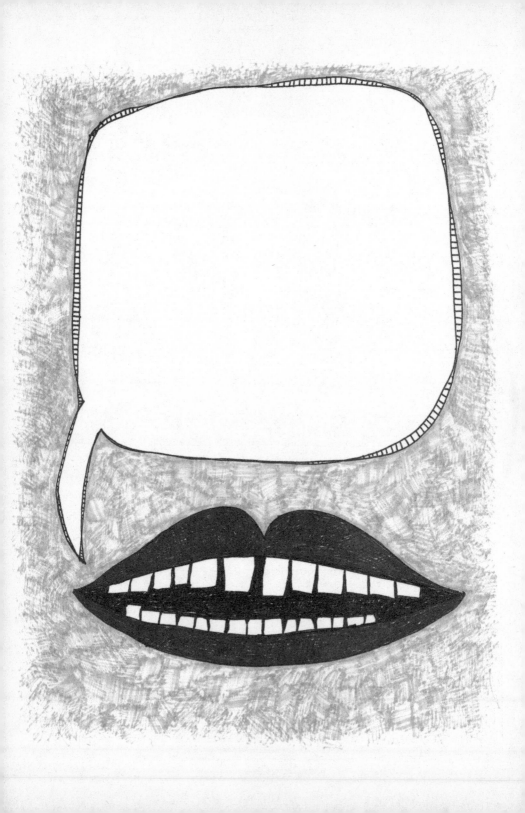

ABOUT THE CONTRIBUTORS

Elise Paschen is the editor of *Poetry Speaks to Children* and coeditor of *Poetry Speaks,* both *New York Times* bestsellers. She is the author of several acclaimed poetry collections of her own, including, most recently, *Bestiary* (Red Hen Press, 2009) and *Infidelities,* winner of the Nicholas Roerich Poetry Prize. A graduate of Harvard University, she holds M.Phil. and D.Phil. degrees from Oxford University. Former Executive Director of the Poetry Society of America, she is the co-founder of *Poetry in Motion,* a nationwide program that places poetry in subways and buses, and co-editor of *Poetry in Motion* and *Poetry in Motion from Coast to Coast.* Dr. Paschen teaches in the Writing Program at The School of the Art Institute of Chicago, and she lives in Chicago with her husband and their two children. Visit her at www.elisepaschen.com.

Series Editor **Dominique Raccah** is founder, president, and publisher of Sourcebooks, a leading independent publisher outside of Chicago. Today Sourcebooks is the world's leading publisher of poetry in book-and-audio form, and also publishes nonfiction and fiction. Raccah was the initial visionary of the book *Poetry Speaks,* seeing it as an interactive, engaging way to experience spoken and written poetry. She later brought poetry to younger readers with the *New York Times* bestseller *Poetry Speaks to Children.*

advisory editors:

Elizabeth Alexander is a poet, essayist, playwright, and teacher born in New York City and raised in Washington, DC. Alexander has degrees from

Yale University and Boston University and completed her Ph.D. in English at the University of Pennsylvania. Most recently, she composed and delivered "Praise Song for the Day" for the inauguration of President Barack Obama, also published as a book from Graywolf Press. She has published five books of poems: *The Venus Hottentot*, *Body of Life*, *Antebellum Dream Book*, *American Sublime*, which was one of three finalists for the Pulitzer Prize and was one of the American Library Association's "Notable Books of the Year," and her first young adult collection (co-authored with Marilyn Nelson), *Miss Crandall's School for Young Ladies and Little Misses of Color* (2008 Connecticut Book Award). Visit her at www.elizabethalexander.net.

Joy Harjo's seven books of poetry include *She Had Some Horses*, *The Woman Who Fell from the Sky*, and *How We Became Human: New and Selected Poems*. Her poetry has garnered many awards including a Lila Wallace-Reader's Digest Award, the New Mexico Governor's Award for Excellence in the Arts, the Lifetime Achievement Award from the Native Writers Circle of the Americas, and the William Carlos Williams Award from the Poetry Society of America. Harjo is also a songwriter and performer, having released four award-winning CDs of original music and performances. She performs internationally, solo and with her band, Joy Harjo and the Arrow Dynamics Band (for which she sings and plays saxophone and flutes). Visit her at www.joyharjo.com.

Brad Leithauser was born in Detroit and graduated from Harvard College and Harvard Law School. He is the author of five novels, a novel in verse (*Darlington's Fall*), five volumes of poetry, a collection of light verse, and a book of essays. His poetry collections include *Curves and Angles*, *The Odd Last Thing She Did*, *The Mail from Anywhere*, *Cats of the Temple*, and *Hundreds of Fireflies*. Among his many awards and honors are a Guggenheim Fellowship, an Ingram Merrill Grant, and a MacArthur Fellowship.

ACKNOWLEDGMENTS

Many thanks to our advisory editors, Joy Harjo, Brad Leithauser, and Elizabeth Alexander, who, as we compiled *Poetry Speaks Who I Am* over these several years, have offered their insights, suggestions, poems, and energy.

We also would like to express gratitude to all the poets who submitted poems to the anthology. Thanks to those writers who also recommended suggestions of their own favorite poems from middle school, particularly: Billy Collins, Toi Derricotte, Annie Finch, Parneshia Jones, Kimiko Hahn, Molly Peacock, Kevin Prufer, Grace Schulman, the late W. D. Snodgrass, Elizabeth Spires, Diane Thiel, Marilyn Waniek, Rosanna Warren, Nancy Willard, and Richard Wilbur. Special gratitude to X. J. Kennedy and to Mary Jo Salter for their ideas and to Edward Hirsch for steering us to the Bar Mitzvah poems of Philip Schultz.

Our thanks to the poets who so graciously took time out of their busy schedules to go into studios across the country to record their work for the CD accompanying this book. These poets have proven again and again that, indeed, poetry speaks. Thanks to all the studios and producers involved in these recordings and special thanks to our friends in public radio and at NPR for the use of several of their studios and for their continual support of poets and poetry.

I also would like to thank Tom Rosenbluth and David Fuder, middle school educators at Francis W. Parker School, with whom I discussed the seeds of this anthology. And gratitude to Stephen Young, Julie Parson Nesbitt, Jenn Morea, Jennifer Levine, Catherine Parnell, and Anndell Quintero for their help, and especially to Isabel Kadish for illuminating the mind of a thirteen-year old.

Thanks to my own family: my husband, Stuart Brainerd, and to our daughter, Alexandra, on the cusp of pre-teendom, and to our son, Stephen, not far behind.

Lastly, immense thanks to the staff at Sourcebooks, particularly my editor, Todd Stocke, who surpasses all expectations of an editor, and who continues to deftly guide these *Poetry Speaks* anthologies from birth to maturity.

PERMISSIONS

AUDIO

Elizabeth Alexander recorded at the Yale Broadcast and Media Center, New Haven, Connecticut.

Marilyn Chin recorded at KPBS Radio, San Diego, California.

Wanda Coleman recorded at Theta Sound Studio, Burbank, California.

Billy Collins recorded at WMFE, Orlando, Florida.

Rita Dove recorded at the Virginia Foundation for the Humanities, Charlottesville, Virginia.

Stephen Dunn recorded at WFWM, Frostburg, Maryland.

Calvin Forbes recorded at Experimental Sound Studio, Chicago, Illinois.

Dana Gioia recorded by Nayna Sasidharan.

Kimiko Hahn, Edward Hirsch, and David Yezzi recorded at Dubway Studios, New York, New York.

Joy Harjo recorded by Larry Mitchell, www.larrymitchell.com.

Parneshia Jones and Elise Paschen recorded at Mystery Street Recording Company, Chicago, Illinois.

X. J. Kennedy recorded by Josh Kennedy.

Rebecca Lauren and Sonia Sanchez recorded at Sine Studios, Baltimore, Maryland.

Marilyn Nelson recorded at Riverway Studio, East Haddam, Connecticut.

Naomi Shihab Nye recorded at Texas Public Radio, San Antonio, Texas.

Rainy Ortiz recorded by Lindsey Bair, Phoenix, Arizona.

Molly Peacock recorded at the CBC, Toronto, Ontario.

Kevin Prufer recorded at KTBG, Warrensburg, Missouri.

Kay Ryan recorded at Studio Jory, Fairfax, California.

Philip Schultz recorded at MonkMusic Productions, East Hampton, New York.

Elizabeth Spires recorded at SoundLocker, Baltimore, Maryland.

Arthur Sze recorded at Santa Fe Community College radio, Santa Fe, New Mexico.

Nancy Willard recorded by Paul Kane.

Bill Zavatsky recorded at Loop Seven, New York, New York.

INDEX